D0572584

T1-AWZ-186

Gregor Mendel:

Genetics Pioneer

by Lynn Van Gorp

Science Contributor
Sally Ride Science
Science Consultants
Thomas R. Ciccone, Science Educator
Ronald Edwards, Science Educator

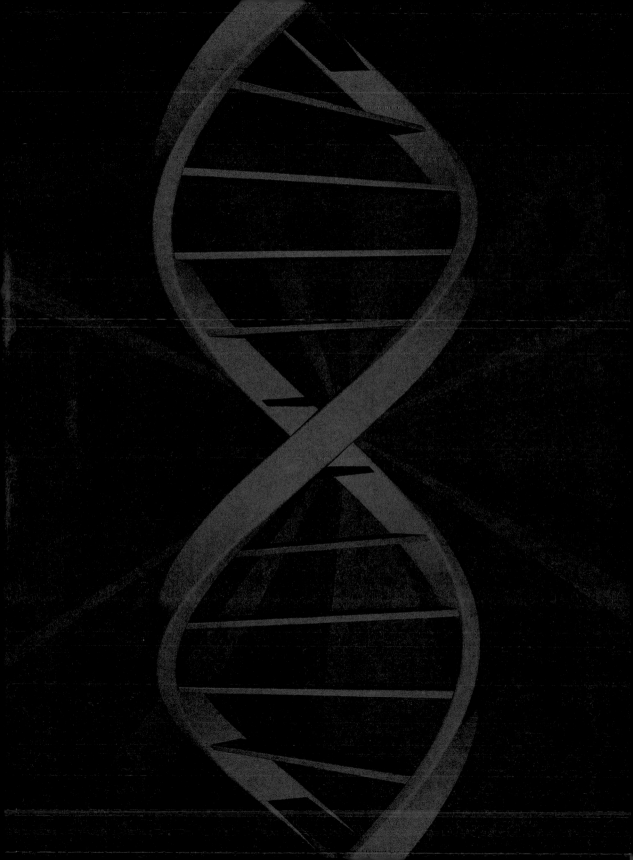

First hardcover edition published in 2009 by
Compass Point Books
151 Good Counsel Drive
P.O. Box 669
Mankato, MN 56002-0669

Editor: Brenda Haugen
Designer: Heidi Thompson
Editorial Contributor: Sue Vander Hook

Art Director: LuAnn Ascheman-Adams
Creative Director: Keith Griffin
Editorial Director: Nick Healy
Managing Editor: Catherine Neitge

 This book was manufactured with paper containing at least 10 percent post-consumer waste.

Library of Congress Cataloging-in-Publication Data
Van Gorp, Lynn.
Gregor Mendel : genetics pioneer / by Lynn Van Gorp.
    p. cm. — (Mission: Science)
 Includes index.
 ISBN 978-0-7565-3963-4 (library binding)
1. Mendel, Gregor, 1822–1884—Juvenile literature.
2. Geneticists—Austria—Biography—Juvenile literature. I. Title.
QH31.M45V36 2009
576.5092—dc22
[B]   2008007725

Visit Compass Point Books on the Internet at *www.compasspointbooks.com*
or e-mail your request to *custserv@compasspointbooks.com*

Table of Contents

Scientist Gregor Johann Mendel's "laboratory" was his garden—a garden filled with a huge variety of pea plants. Mendel experimented for eight years with about 28,000 plants.

Mendel had a beautiful garden, but he was much more than a gardener. He was a scientist who questioned and experimented until he opened the door to the world of genetics— the study of how characteristics are passed from one generation to the next.

But Mendel would never know how important his findings were. Sixteen years after his death in 1884, some scientists took a serious look at his work, and the science of genetics was launched. Mendel's discoveries would be called Mendel's laws of heredity. And Mendel would come to be known as the father of genetics.

An illustration from the seed catalog *Album Benary* shows a variety of characteristics of the pea plants Mendel studied.

Johann Mendel was born in 1822 in Heinzendorf, a small town in what was then the Austrian Empire but now is a part of the Czech Republic. Mendel's parents were poor farmers who didn't even own the land they farmed. Mendel's life was hard. When he was young, he worked as a gardener, but he wanted a better life.

At that time, it was nearly impossible for poor children to go to school. Although Mendel's parents had little money, they were able to come up with enough to pay for their son's education. He attended

the Philosophical Institute in Olomouc. When his father was injured and unable to work, Mendel got financial help from his two sisters.

In 1843, the 21-year-old Mendel became a monk. He entered the Abbey of St. Thomas and was given the name Gregor.

St. Thomas was a teaching monastery in Brno. It was a place of learning and scientific inquiry, and the opportunities were a dream come true for Mendel.

Mendel was born near Prague, which is now the capital and largest city in the Czech Republic.

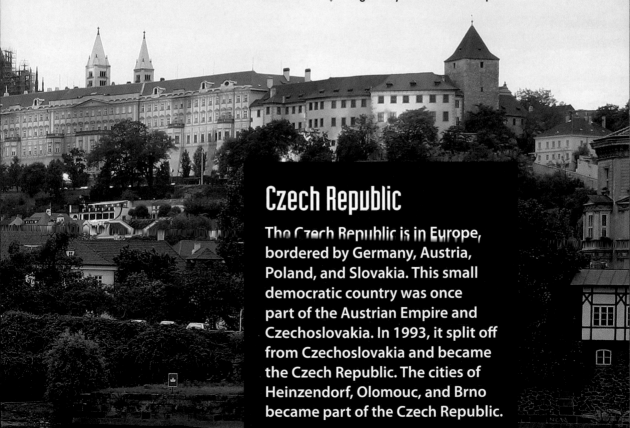

Czech Republic

The Czech Republic is in Europe, bordered by Germany, Austria, Poland, and Slovakia. This small democratic country was once part of the Austrian Empire and Czechoslovakia. In 1993, it split off from Czechoslovakia and became the Czech Republic. The cities of Heinzendorf, Olomouc, and Brno became part of the Czech Republic.

Monk and Teacher

At St. Thomas, Mendel got up every morning at 6 and went straight to the library to study. He had many interests—physics, math, astronomy, meteorology, botany, and more. During the day, he taught Latin, Greek, and math to other students. But when he took a test to become an official teacher, he didn't pass it.

However, Mendel's teachers recognized what a bright student he was. They made it possible for him to attend the University of Vienna to get a teaching diploma. Although Mendel never got that diploma, he was inspired to study how plants and animals grew. It would change the course of his life.

Mendel lived at the Abbey of St. Thomas from the age of 21 until his death at the age of 61.

Monasteries such as one in Meteora, Greece, have been centers for learning for centuries.

Monasteries

A monastery is a building where monks live to fulfill their religious vows. Various religions have monasteries in many parts of the world. Committed people separate themselves from society and live their lives in monasteries. The monks of Mendel's monastery belonged to the Roman Catholic Augustinian order, which observes the rules found in the writings of St. Augustine.

For thousands of years, people have also gone to monasteries to learn. Many well-known scientists have studied and taught in monasteries. Some monasteries also have given shelter to travelers and aid to the poor.

University Days

Mendel studied at the University of Vienna for two years. He was especially interested in the work of a biologist there named Frank Unger. Biologists study the science of life and living things. Unger had fascinating ideas about inheritance. He looked at nature and saw similarities and differences in the way animals and plants grew. Mendel had seen the same things when he was working on the family farm, where he had helped his father breed fruit trees.

Although Mendel was a bright, inquisitive student, he didn't do well on tests. In fact, he got physically ill when he had to take an exam. As a result, Mendel decided to

⬆ Mendel (back row, right) posed with a group of monks and teachers in 1865.

The University of Vienna, one of the oldest universities in Europe, opened in 1365.

Test Anxiety

Mendel was believed to have test anxiety, a fear of taking tests that can make a person physically ill. He was so afraid of taking tests that he usually couldn't even take them.

withdraw from the university. Even though he didn't finish, he learned valuable research skills while he was at the university. He learned how to perform experiments and analyze results.

Mendel returned to the monastery, where he taught physics. Although he wasn't allowed to teach biology, he could do research, which is exactly what he did. For the next eight years, he studied and experimented on peas in the monastery garden.

Garden Peas

Peas were a common vegetable at that time. They were also easy to raise and had a short breeding, or reproduction, time. So they were good for experimenting.

bloomed on the young plants were different colors.

Most important for Mendel, peas could be cross-pollinated, which means one variety could be bred with another. Mendel bought pea seeds from people who lived in the area. The popular vegetable was everywhere. It is believed that Mendel started with 34 varieties of pea plants. Over time, that number grew to at least 28,000 plants, all of which Mendel tested and studied.

A wide variety of peas grew in the area. There were tall plants and short plants; peas with green pods and others with yellow pods. Some of the pea pods were fat and inflated, while others were flat. The peas inside might be round, or they could be wrinkled. Even the flowers that

Mendel crossbred, or mixed, thousands of varieties of pea plants. This allowed him to make predictions about what the new varieties would look like. He first mixed a tall plant with a short plant. He noticed that the new plants were all tall. But the next time, when he mixed a new tall plant with a short

Peas and People

From Mendel's study of garden peas, scientists were able to understand how people's characteristics are passed down from generation to generation.

plant, about two-thirds of the next generation of plants were tall, but a third of them were short.

Through his research and observations, Mendel was also able to explain how traits passed from one generation of pea plants to the next. These findings would eventually be called Mendel's laws of heredity.

Mendel's Experiment

Before Mendel, many people believed in the theory of blending. They thought offspring had traits—personal characteristics—that were a mixture of their parents' traits. In other words, if a mother had blue eyes and a father had green eyes, their children would have blue-green eyes. Mendel was the first to find that some traits show up in offspring without any blending.

Mendel believed the results of his experiments would be valid if he studied thousands of plants. He thought that if he studied fewer plants, his findings might be the result of chance or luck. By studying thousands of plants, his results would be proven.

First Mendel looked at seven traits of his pea plants. Each trait had two phenotypes, or differences he could see.

An experiment that crossed yellow wrinkled peas (top left) with green round peas (top right) produced a mixture of colored peas.

Reproduction

Reproduction is the process of making offspring. Plants as well as animals reproduce their own kind. People make people, dogs make dogs, and trees make trees. When living things reproduce, they pass their genes, or hereditary material, to their offspring. Genes, which are found in the cells, are what make a living thing what it is.

People get their genes from both of their parents. A person's body follows the instructions given by the genes. These instructions tell the body everything, from what the person's eye color should be to how big his or her feet should grow.

Whether it is a person, a cow, a monkey, a pineapple, a blueberry, or an elm tree, a living thing has traits that are passed down from the parents.

Traits Mendel Compared

Characteristic	Dominant Trait	Recessive Trait
stem length	tall	short
flower position	top	side
seed shape	round	wrinkled
seed color	yellow	green
flower color	purple	white
pod shape	puffed	pinched
pod color	green	yellow

Dominant and Recessive Alleles

For two years, Mendel grew many varieties of peas and made sure their offspring were always the same. He didn't want any differences between the parent plants and their offspring—yet.

Mendel observed the traits of each plant and checked to see whether they were the same as the traits of the parent plants. Then Mendel began crossbreeding varieties to produce hybrids, or new species. For example, he transferred pollen from the flower of a yellow pea plant to the flower of a green pea plant.

Year after year, Mendel grew many generations of hybrid peas. He noted how each hybrid changed and what traits showed up or disappeared from generation to generation. Some traits appeared often. He called those dominant traits. Other

traits disappeared for a while and showed up in later generations. He called those recessive traits.

Scientists didn't understand Mendel's findings for a long time. But eventually they grasped what he had learned about heredity. They discovered that the principles apply to animals as well as plants. For every trait, each parent passes on one gene to a child. There is a gene that determines the color of your hair, a gene that decides whether your earlobes will be attached or unattached, and so on.

Scientists also one day understood that each gene has two alleles, or alternate forms. Some alleles are dominant, and others are recessive. A recessive trait shows up only if both parents pass on a gene with two recessive alleles.

Orchid farmers often harvest pollen from one plant to breed it with another.

18

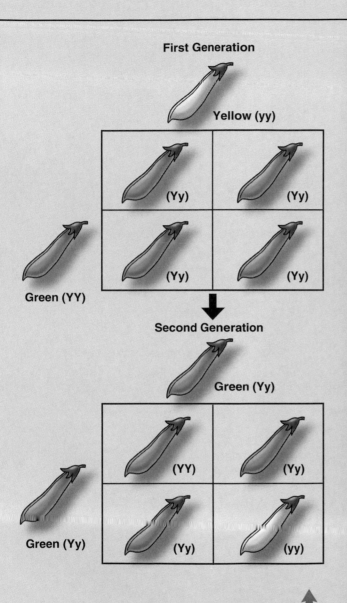

First Generation

Yellow (yy)

(Yy) (Yy)

(Yy) (Yy)

Green (YY)

↓

Second Generation

Green (Yy)

(YY) (Yy)

(Yy) (yy)

Green (Yy)

↑

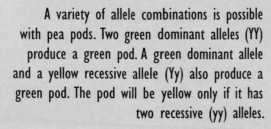

A variety of allele combinations is possible with pea pods. Two green dominant alleles (YY) produce a green pod. A green dominant allele and a yellow recessive allele (Yy) also produce a green pod. The pod will be yellow only if it has two recessive (yy) alleles.

Eye Color

Some parents like to guess what color their baby's eyes will be. Eye color is determined partly by how much melanin is in the iris of the eye. Melanin is a substance that provides color to eyes or skin. Brown eyes have a lot of melanin, while blue eyes have very little.

Genes control the amount of melanin a person has. Most people have dark eyes, ranging from brown to nearly black. Blue eyes occur only when neither parent gives the baby a brown gene.

Unpopular Ideas

In 1865, when Mendel was 43 years old, he presented the results of his research at a meeting of scientists. The scientists were polite, but they had little reaction to his work. They didn't understand the importance of his findings and barely took notice. His research was very different from other scientific work being done at that time.

The following year, Mendel published his report, "Experiments with Plant Hybrids," in a scientific journal. Still no one took notice. Unfortunately, Mendel had few other opportunities to share his work. Over the next 35 years, his findings

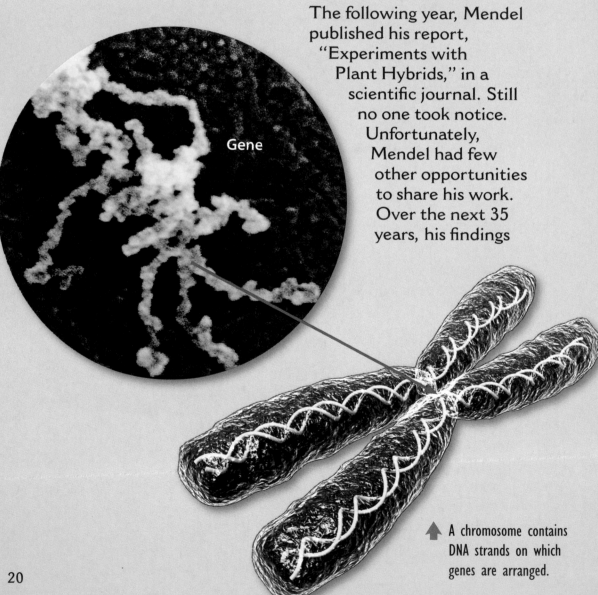

Gene

A chromosome contains DNA strands on which genes are arranged.

were referred to only a few times. People even criticized his work.

In 1868, Mendel became abbot, or head, of the monastery, and he had little time for scientific research. On January 6, 1884, Mendel died at the age of 61. He had received no scientific awards or recognition for his work in genetics. At that time, he was remembered only as a monk and a teacher. But in the early 1900s, scientists began to understand the importance of his work.

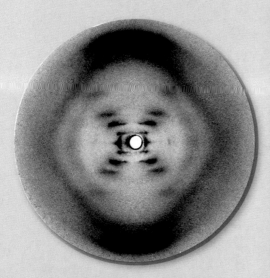

Franklin's photograph of DNA

Rosalind Franklin (1920-1958)

Rosalind Franklin was another scientist who died before people recognized her work. She produced the first clear photograph of DNA, the chemical of which genes are made. She died of cancer in 1958 at the age of 37.

Two other scientists, James D. Watson and Francis Crick, used her findings and photograph as part of their own research. In 1962, Watson and Crick, along with another scientist, Maurice Wilkins, received the Nobel Prize in medicine for their work in mapping the structure of DNA. Franklin was not mentioned. However, the scientists later acknowledged Franklin's work and its importance to their research. Today the world is aware of Franklin and the contribution she made to genetics.

Mendel's Contribution

Sixteen years after Mendel's death, the science of genetics was born. In 1900, scientists rediscovered his work and began to study his research. They also realized how important his conclusions were. Mendel gave the world important information about how characteristics are passed from one generation to the next.

Mendel explained how each trait is determined by "factors" that are inherited. Each trait has a pair of factors, one from each parent. One factor is dominant, while the other is recessive. His experiments showed that some traits do not always show up, but they can still be passed to other generations. Mendel's laws of heredity

DNA

A baby's first cell has a code with all the instructions needed to make that baby. The first cell has tiny chromosomes inside. Half of the chromosomes came from the mother's egg cell, and the other half came from the father's sperm cell. The chromosomes carry genes, which are made of a chemical called deoxyribonucleic acid—DNA for short.

Chromosomes are so small that they can be seen only when they bunch together.

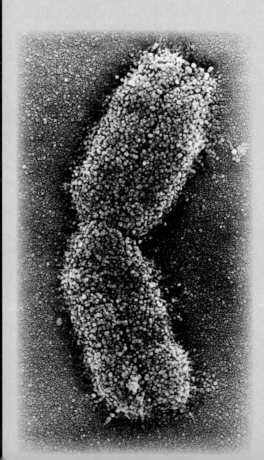

laid the foundation for many more discoveries in the science of genetics.

Mendel used a microscope in his research, but as microscopes improved, scientists made more discoveries about genetics. They found chromosomes in the centers of cells. What they saw were threadlike structures that hold thousands of genes, the basic units of heredity. They found that humans have 46 chromosomes, while horses have 64, dogs have 78, and mosquitoes have six. And they confirmed Mendel's finding that parents pass traits to their offspring, whether the offspring is a child, a chicken, a donkey, a watermelon, or a pea plant.

Genes

Genes determine the color of an animal's coat. Many genes interact to determine what color it will be. That is why there are so many color patterns in the fur of cats, dogs, and other animals.

What Are the Odds?

Mendel's findings answered a lot of questions about inherited traits. What are the odds that you will have straight hair, brown eyes, dimples, or a tongue that will curl up into funny shapes? Mendel's laws explained the odds. Let's take the ability to roll your tongue as an example.

Being able to roll your tongue is a dominant trait. Both of your parents have two genes that relate to tongue rolling. They might have two dominant genes, two recessive genes, or one of each. If one of your parents has two dominant tongue-rolling genes, you will receive a dominant gene from that parent. If your other parent has two recessive tongue-rolling genes, you will receive a recessive gene from that parent. But if they have one of each gene, you may get

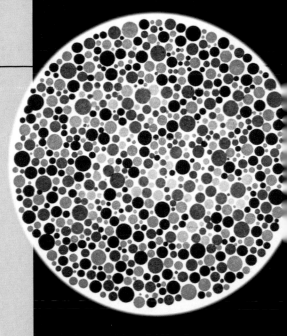

either a dominant or a recessive gene. There's no way to tell.

If you happen to receive two dominant genes, you will be able to roll your tongue. You will also be able to roll your tongue if you receive a dominant gene and a recessive gene. The only way you won't be a tongue roller is if you receive two recessive tongue-rolling genes.

Color Blindness

Color blindness is an inherited trait. People who are colorblind cannot see certain colors. About one in 12 men is colorblind; only one in 200 women has the condition.

Red/green color blindness is the most common type. Someone with normal color vision will see the number 74 in the above dot pattern. Someone with red/green color blindness will see either the number 21 or no number at all in the dot pattern.

Dominant and Recessive Traits

	Dominant Traits	Recessive Traits
eye color	brown	gray, green, hazel, blue
hair	dark	blonde, light
	non-red	red
	curly	straight
facial features	dimples	no dimples
	freckles	no freckles

Remember: Both parents need to pass the recessive trait in order for their child to inherit it. Do you have any recessive traits?

Mendel's Legacy

More than 50 years after Mendel shared his findings, a Dutch scientist named Hugo De Vries did the same type of research on hybrid plants. In 1889, De Vries wrote a book titled *Intracellular Pangenesis*. In it he suggested that specific traits in an organism come in particles called pangenes. The word was later shortened to genes.

Most of his conclusions were the same as Mendel's, except De Vries came up with a theory of gene mutation, a change in the

▲ Hugo De Vries' experiments with pea plants were similar to Mendel's.

gene. He thought a gene could change and instantly alter the offspring. He said a mutation would make a change in the next generation; the change wouldn't have to wait for future generations.

Since then, other scientists have studied pea plants. Some of their findings back up Mendel's work, and others disagree with Mendel's conclusions.

Mendel's Microscope

Mendel used a simple light microscope to study peas. Because his microscope was not very powerful, he couldn't see chromosomes, the parts of a cell that contain the genetic material. Today microscopes are still an essential part of research. Major scientific discoveries have been made because microscopes have become more powerful with greater detail and three-dimensional images.

Did You Know?

In 1892, a German botanist named Carl Correns (1864–1933) studied plant genetics. Even though Correns didn't know about Gregor Mendel's findings, he came up with the same results.

Scientist Barbara McClintock learned new things about genetics from studying corn. Her work was a lot like Mendel's. She had a garden near her laboratory where she planted different kinds of corn so she could breed them and make new types. Some of the plants came from Central America and South America, where she loved to travel.

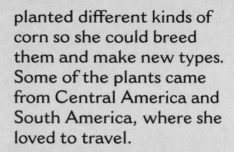

For years, no one believed the conclusions McClintock made about corn. But that didn't stop her from studying. She never gave up. Finally she made a surprising discovery. She found a special gene that can swap places with other genes. In 1983, she was awarded the Nobel Prize in medicine for her discovery of what were called "mobile genetic elements." McClintock also enjoyed teaching, which she did until she died at the age of 90.

Scientists today are still studying genetics, building on the foundations laid by scientists such as Gregor Mendel. These scientists

look at chromosomes, genes, DNA, alleles, and other aspects of genetics, searching for more answers to their questions about heredity. And who knows which scientist will be the next to discover another piece of the genetic puzzle?

Answer the Question

It has been said that Barbara McClintock could take an entire afternoon to answer one question. Then, after talking for hours, she would say, "We'd better stop now—you look tired!"

In Her Words

Barbara McClintock once said about her career in science: "It might seem unfair to reward a person for having so much pleasure over the years."

29

Name:	Gregor Johann Mendel
Date of birth:	July 20, 1822
Nationality:	Austrian
Birthplace:	Heinzendorf, Austrian Empire (now Hynice, Czech Republic)
Parents:	Anton and Rosine Mendel
Children:	None
Date of death:	January 6, 1884
Place of burial:	Brno, Austria-Hungary (now Czech Republic)
Field of study:	Genetics
Known as:	Father of genetics
Contributions to science:	Discovered modern genetics
Publication:	"Experiments with Plant Hybrids"

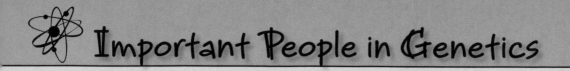

William Bateson (1861–1926)
British geneticist who helped establish the new science of genetics in 1900; he was the first scientist to use the word *genetics*

Walther Flemming (1843–1905)
German scientist who investigated cell division and how chromosomes distribute to the second nucleus; he called the process mitosis

Rosalind Franklin (1920–1958)
English scientist who made significant contributions to understanding the structure of DNA

Barbara McClintock (1902–1992)
Scientist who won the Nobel Prize in medicine in 1983 for her work on genetic research

Karl Nägeli (1817–1891)
Swiss botanist who studied plant cells and stained chromosomes to see them better under a microscope; he is credited with being the first to observe the process of cell growth and division

Reginald Punnett (1875–1967)
British geneticist who helped establish the new science of genetics in 1900; best known for his Punnett square, a tool used to predict the probability of a particular trait appearing

Walter Sutton (1877–1916)
American scientist who developed the chromosome theory of inheritance, which states that both parents pass chromosomes to their offspring

James D. Watson (1928–   ), **Francis Crick** (1916–2004), and **Maurice Wilkins** (1916–2004)
Scientists who were jointly awarded the 1962 Nobel Prize in medicine for their discovery of the double-helix structure of DNA

1333 First botanical garden is founded in Venice, Italy

1580 Prospero Alpini finds that plants have male and female sexes

1682 Nehemiah Grew describes the types of plant stem and root tissues and identifies male and female parts of flowering plants

1694 Rudolph Jakob Camerarius determines the male and female plant reproductive organs

1763 Joseph Gottlieb Kölreuter conducts the first fertilization experiments on plants using animal pollinators

1844 Karl Nägeli sees the process of cell growth and division under a microscope

1856 Mendel begins studying pea plants; he discovers that plants pass along dominant and recessive traits

1882 Walther Flemming publishes a book that illustrates and describes cell division

1900 Reginald Punnett and William Bateson establish the new science of genetics at Cambridge University

1901 Hugo De Vries determines that changes in a species occur in jumps, which he calls mutations

1902 Walter Sutton determines that chromosomes may be the carriers of inherited characteristics; he develops the chromosome theory of heredity

1905 Female mammals are found to have two X chromosomes; male mammals are found to have an XY pair

1953 DNA structure is discovered by James Watson and Francis Crick; their work is based on the work of Rosalind Franklin

1954 Scientists discover that humans have 46 chromosomes

1965 Hans Ris and Walter Plaut discover DNA in the chloroplasts of algae

1969 First single gene is isolated

1980 Scientists transfer a gene from one mouse to another and discover the gene still functions

1983 Barbara McClintock wins the Nobel Prize in medicine for her work in genetics

1986 First genetically engineered organisms (tobacco) are grown in Wisconsin

1988 First genetically engineered mouse is developed

allele—alternate form of the same gene

analyze—examine something carefully in order to understand it

astronomy—study of planets, stars, and space

biology—science of life and living things

botanist—scientist who studies plant life

botany—scientific study of plants

breed—to produce offspring

chromosome—threadlike structure in the nucleus of a living cell that carries the genes

crossbreed—produce offspring by the mating of genetically different varieties or species

cross-pollinate—transfer the pollen from one flower to another flower, allowing the genetic traits to mix in the offspring

DNA (deoxyribonucleic acid)—chemical of which genes are made

dominant allele—allele form of a gene most likely to produce a trait in offspring

fertilize—reproduce either by the union of male and female sex cells (animals) or by pollination (plants)

gene—basic unit of heredity

generation—all the offspring from one stage of descent from a common ancestor

genetics—branch of science that deals with heredity and genetic variations

heredity—genetic background of a plant or animal

hybrid—plant or animal that has been bred from two different species

inheritance—transmission of characteristics from parent to offspring

1992 Oldest organism known to exist is discovered in Michigan; it is a 1,500-year-old fungus covering 30 acres (12 hectares) underground

1994 Genetically engineered tomatoes that ripen more slowly are introduced into the marketplace

1996 Dolly, a female sheep, is the first animal cloned; she dies in 2003

2003 The Human Genome Project is completed

2007 Scientists discover a gene in a variety of rice that allows the rice plant to grow better in places where the soil isn't rich in nutrients

2008 Researchers study the genetics of maize in order to find ways to improve the crop's level of vitamin A; this will improve the health of people in Africa and Latin America, where maize is a large part of their diet

iris—round, colored part of the eye around the pupil

melanin—substance that gives color to eyes and skin

meteorology—study of the earth's climate and weather

monastery—building where monks live

mutation—change in a gene resulting in a new biological trait or characteristic

Nobel Prize—award given each year for achievement in chemistry, literature, physics, physiology or medicine, economics, or world peace

offspring—descendants of a person, animal, or plant

phenotype—visible traits determined by the genes in an organism

physics—science dealing with matter and energy

recessive allele—allele form of a gene most unlikely to appear in offspring

reproduction—process by which organisms produce other organisms of the same kind

trait—distinguishing feature or genetically determined characteristic

Day, Trevor. *Genetics*. San Diego: Blackbirch Press, 2004.

George, Linda. *Gene Therapy*. San Diego: Blackbirch Press, 2003.

Glimm, Adele. *Gene Hunter: The Story of Neuropsychologist Nancy Wexler*. New York: Franklin Watts, 2005.

Stille, Darlene. *Genetics: A Living Blueprint*. Minneapolis: Compass Point Books, 2006.

Walker, Richard. *Genes and DNA*. Boston: Kingfisher, 2003.

On the Web

For more information on this topic, use FactHound.

1. Go to *www.facthound.com*

2. Type in this book ID: 0756539633

3. Click on the *Fetch It* button.

FactHound will find the best Web sites for you.

Index

Lynn Van Gorp

Lynn Van Gorp graduated with a master of science degree from the University of Calgary, Canada, and did additional graduate work at the University of Washington, Seattle, and the University of California, Irvine. She has taught for more than 30 years, at the elementary and middle-school levels and at the university level. Her educational focus areas include science, reading, and technology. She has written a number of student- and teacher-based curriculum-related publications.

Image Credits